Wheat Free Livin'

Lunch Cookbook

All Rights Reserved. No part of this publication may be reproduced in any form or by any means, including scanning, photocopying, or otherwise without prior written permission of the copyright holder. Copyright © 2014

INTRODUCTION

Wheat has recently been identified as quite the instigator of trouble within the human body. From causing what is known as the "wheat belly", to intestinal damage and even skin problems, going without wheat is sounding like a better and better idea. Removing wheat can be easier said than done, because most foods in restaurants and stores serve wheat as one of the main food groups. It has been on the food pyramid for as long as I can remember! So, making this shift in eating can get some funny responses from people.

However, with a little planning and preparation, these recipes will change even the most outspoken critic of wheat-free eating. Each of these contains a balanced supply of nutrients for the body, providing adequate calories, fats, protein and carbohydrates. When looking at the facts, bread is not needed to keep the body in its optimum health.

Enjoy experimenting with these recipes for delicious dishes and watch to see what happens with your health. Many people and researchers are finding it easier to shed extra pounds, people are feeling increased energy levels and stomach irritation is ceasing. Be sure to pay careful attention to the ingredients when you are shopping to ensure that all follow the wheat free instructions and enjoy!

Table of Contents

Squash with Sliced Mushroom

Zucchini Onion Rolls

Avocado & Tomato Pizza

Red & Yellow Pepper Pizza

Easy Spicy Eggplant Dish

Nutty Harvest Boat

Cucumber Raft

Ratatouille Riverboat

Fruitychicken Melonboat

Barreling Down the River

Red Wrap

Spicy Seafruit Wraps

Dragonchicken Wraps

Eggplant Chicken Burgers

Chickenfish Wraps

Mangospice Chicken Soup

Earthroot Soup

Omelet Soup

Trail Mix Soup

Honeyfruit Soup

Squash with Sliced Mushroom

Prep time: 15-20 minutes

Cook time: approx 20 minutes

Serves: 2

INGREDIENTS

1 large yellow squash

½ pound organic grass-fed ground turkey

2 tbsp extra virgin olive oil

4 baby portobella mushrooms

2 cloves garlic

2 small tomatoes

12 leaves fresh basil

12 oz organic additive-free tomato sauce

3 oz olive tapenade

INSTRUCTIONS

1. Mince the garlic and cut the yellow squash into 12 slices. Cut tomatoes into 12 slices. Slice mushrooms into 12 total slices.

2. Sautee ½ pound ground turkey in 1 tbsp extra virgin olive oil in a saucepan until no longer pink. Then add minced garlic and sautee 2-3 minutes.

3. Add 12 oz organic additive-free tomato sauce and sautee until it bubbles. Remove from heat.

4. Sautee sliced mushrooms in a pan with 1 tbsp extra virgin olive oil until light brown, about 2-3 minutes.

5. For each slice of yellow squash, layer with olive tapenade, then tomato, then meat sauce, then mushroom, then basil. Serve.

Zucchini Onion Rolls

Prep time: 15 minutes

Cook time: 10 minutes

Serves: 2

INGREDIENTS

1 large zucchini

2-3 cloves garlic

6.5 oz artichoke hearts

½ medium onion

6 slices low sodium organic grass-fed turkey bacon

12 oz organic additive-free tomato sauce

½ green pepper

¼ tsp dried basil

¼ tsp dried oregano

¼ tsp ground black pepper

INSTRUCTIONS

1. Cut zucchini lengthwise into 8 pliable sheets. Mince the garlic and dice the onion, green pepper and artichoke.

2. Sautee bacon until it's browned. Remove the bacon from the pan and crumble. Set aside.

3. Put green pepper and onion in the pan and sautee for 2 minutes. Add garlic and sautee for another minute. Add artichoke and red sauce and bring to a bubble, about 5 minutes.

4. Add crumbled bacon and dried basil, oregano and ground black pepper to the pan. Thoroughly stir together.

5. For each slice of zucchini, spread cooked mixture evenly across the top and then roll up. Serve.

Avocado & Tomato Pizza

Prep time: 7 minutes

Cook time: 3-4 minutes

Serves: 2

INGREDIENTS

2 avocados

2 low sodium organic grass-fed turkey sauce links (pre-cooked)

½ cup chopped pineapple

1 large tomato

1 tbsp extra virgin olive oil

INSTRUCTIONS

1. Slice avocados in half. Remove the pit and the peel and set aside.

2. Dice the sausage and tomato into small pieces and add into a pan with extra virgin olive oil along with chopped pineapple. Heat through, about 3-4 minutes.

3. Place two halves of avocado on 1 plate each. Evenly distribute the sauteed ingredients into each avocado. Drizzle the remaining mixture over each avocado. Serve.

Red & Yellow Pepper Pizza

Prep time: 15 minutes

Cook time: 15 minutes

Serves: 2

INGREDIENTS

Pizza

1 red pepper

1 yellow pepper

1 small red onion

1 low-sodium cooked organic grass-fed chicken sausage link

1 cup broccoli florets

1 tbsp extra virgin olive oil

Pesto

1 packed cup fresh basil

¼ cup extra virgin olive oil

¼ cup walnuts

3 cloves garlic

¼ tsp Celtic sea salt

¼ tsp ground black pepper

INSTRUCTIONS

1. Cut the peppers in half. Remove the stems, cores and seeds. Line a baking sheet with aluminum foil and place the peppers in it skin side up. Put peppers under the broiler and leave them there until the skin has begun to turn black and shriveled.

2. Remove peppers from oven, place in a plastic bag and place in refrigerator until cool.

3. Peel the skins off the peppers and throw them away.

4. Slice the onion into half moon slices and slice the chicken sausage link into twelve thin slices. Place the onion, sausage slices and broccoli florets with 1 tbsp extra virgin olive oil in a saucepan over medium heat for 4 minutes until vegetables are tender crisp and meat is slightly browned.

5. Place all the pesto ingredients in a food processor and blend until smooth.

6. Put two halves of roasted pepper on a dish, one red and one yellow, open side up. Using a spoon, spread pesto evenly inside each pepper half. Evenly distribute broccoli, onion, and sausage over the tops.

7. Serve.

Easy Spicy Eggplant Dish

Prep time: 10 minutes

Cook time: 8 minutes

Serves: 2

INGREDIENTS

½ large eggplant cut lengthwise

4 asparagus stalks

2 cloves garlic

1 yellow tomato

2 tsp fresh cilantro

2 tbsp extra virgin olive oil

1 cup organic red sauce

INSTRUCTIONS

1. In a medium saucepan, heat the red sauce on low and keep hot.

2. Slice the eggplant into ½ inch slices, 8 slices total. Heat 1 ½ extra virgin olive oil in a frying pan on medium heat. Cook the eggplant two minutes on one side and another two minutes on the other side. Transfer to a plate.

3. Add ½ tbsp to the pan. Slice the garlic. Rinse the asparagus and cut each asparagus stalk into 3 equal lengths.

4. Add garlic and asparagus to pan and sautee until asparagus is tender.

5. Dice yellow tomato and cilantro and mix together.

6. Place four slices of eggplant on each plate. Spoon red sauce over each slice. Cover with tomato/cilantro mixture and evenly distribute asparagus and garlic cloves.

7. Serve.

Nutty Harvest Boat

Prep time: 10 minutes

Cook time: 6-8 minutes

Serves: 2

INGREDIENTS

2 delicata squash

6 oz bag of organic coleslaw mix

3 scallions

1 cup slivered almonds

¼ cup sunflower seeds

1 medium carrot

1 mandarin orange

2 celery stalks

2 tbsp raw unfiltered honey

2 tbsp vinegar

¼ cup extra virgin olive oil

INSTRUCTIONS

1. Chop the scallions and celery and shred the carrot. Peel the orange.
   Cut the delicata squash in half lengthwise and dispose of the seeds.

2. Place the squash in a microwave safe dish cut side up. Put 1 tbsp of water in the bottom of the dish. Cover and microwave on high for 6 minutes. Test with fork and if the fork doesn't go in easily, continue microwaving until it does.

3. In a medium sized mixing bowl, placing the larger ingredients in first, combine scallions, slivered almonds, sunflower seeds, carrot, orange slices and celery. Mix well.

4. In a small bowl, mix the honey, vinegar and extra virgin olive oil. Pour this mixture over the other ingredients and mix.

5. Scoop this mixture evenly into each half of delicata squash. Place two halves on each plate.

6. Serve.

Cucumber Raft

Prep time: 20 minutes

Cook time: 15 minutes

Serves: 2

INGREDIENTS

2 cucumbers

2 cups shredded lettuce

1 medium sized tomato

1 cup cooked quinoa

½ avocado

½ cup grapes

¼ cup chopped walnuts

2 tbsp raspberry vinaigrette

INSTRUCTIONS

1. Peel the cucumbers and cut in half lengthwise. Scoop out seeds and discard. Dice the tomato and avocado and cut the grapes in half.

2. Put ¼ cup of the cooked quinoa inside the hollow core of each slice of cucumber. Then distribute the following ingredients evenly across each cucumber in the following order: shredded lettuce,

tomato, avocado, grapes and chopped walnuts. Drizzle the raspberry vinaigrette over the tops of each.

3. Serve.

Ratatouille Riverboat

Prep time: 10 minutes

Cook time: 1 hour

Serves: 2

INGREDIENTS

1 large eggplant

1 medium zucchini

½ onion

1 cup mushrooms

½ green bell pepper

1 tomato

1 cup vegetable stock

2 cloves garlic

2 tbsp extra virgin olive oil

½ tsp thyme

¼ tsp parsley

INSTRUCTIONS

1. Preheat oven to 400 degrees.

2. Cut the eggplant in half lengthwise and scoop out the seeds, leaving an oblong bowl through the middle of each. Brush with 1 tbsp extra virgin olive oil. Place them cut side down on a baking sheet lined with parchment paper. Place in the oven for one hour.

3. Chop the green bell pepper, tomato, zucchini and onion. Slice the mushrooms. Combine all these ingredients in a medium saucepan with 1 tbsp extra virgin olive oil. Saute over medium heat for 4 minutes.

4. Add vegetable stock, thyme and parsley to the saucepan and let simmer until some of the liquid cooks down, approximately 10 minutes.

5. Place each half of eggplant on a plate and scoop out the vegetable mixture over the top of each.

Fruitychicken Melonboat

Prep time: 20 minutes

Cook time: 10 minutes

Serves: 2

INGREDIENTS

1 small watermelon

½ cup black raspberries

½ cup Juan canary melon

1 organic grass-fed chicken breast

1 shallot

2 clementines

½ green pepper

1 tbsp extra virgin olive oil

INSTRUCTIONS

1. Cube the Juan canary melon. Peel the clementine and divide into wedges. Chop the green pepper and shallot. Cut the watermelon in half, scoop out the flesh and chop it up. Set rind aside.

2. Grill the chicken for 2-3 minutes on each side until no longer pink. Chop the chicken into cubes and set aside.

3. In a small pan, combine extra virgin olive oil, chopped pepper and shallot. Sautee for 4 minutes.

4. Place all the ingredients in a medium bowl and mix evenly with a spoon. Scoop half the ingredients into each watermelon bowl. Serve.

Barreling Down the River

Prep time: 10 minutes

Cook time: 15 minutes

Serves: 2

INGREDIENTS

2 red bell peppers

1 green bell pepper

1 filet of haddock

1 medium onion

1 medium tomato

1 can organic tomato paste

½ tsp oregano

¼ tsp Celtic sea salt

¼ tsp ground black pepper

2 tbsp extra virgin olive oil

INSTRUCTIONS

1. Chop the tops off the red bell peppers and core them, removing the seeds and white fleshy interior. Set aside. Chop the green bell pepper and onion. Dice the tomato.

2. In a medium saucepan heat the green bell pepper and onion in extra virgin olive oil over medium heat for 4 minutes. Add the tomato and the can of tomato paste, stir and let simmer for another 5 minutes.

3. In a frying pan, heat 1 tbsp extra virgin olive oil over medium heat and add the fish filet. Cook until the fish flakes easily, about 5-7 minutes, turning once.

4. Add the filet to the saucepan with all remaining ingredients and seasonings, stirring the ingredients together and breaking up the filet into smaller pieces.

5. Scoop the contents into the bell peppers and serve, one on each plate.

Red Wrap

Prep time: 20 minutes

Serves: 2

INGREDIENTS

Wrap

6 slices organic grass-fed deli turkey

½ red bell pepper

6 cherry tomatoes

½ avocado

6 arugula leaves

Pesto

½ packed cup fresh basil

2 tbsp extra virgin olive oil

2 tbsp almonds

1 clove garlic

¼ tsp Celtic sea salt

INSTRUCTIONS

1. Chop the red bell pepper. Mash the avocado.

2. Combine the pesto ingredients in a food processor and puree. Set aside.

3. Stack 3 slices of turkey and spread half the pesto across the top. Across the middle, lay ¼ cup chopped red bell pepper, half the avocado mash, 3 cherry tomatoes and 3 arugula leaves. Repeat this process for the other 3 slices of turkey and wrap them both up, securing with toothpicks. Serve.

Spicy Seafruit Wraps

Prep time: 15 minutes

Serves: 2

INGREDIENTS

4 sheets of Nori

1 can of tuna fish

1 tbsp extra virgin olive oil

1 tsp dried mustard

2 scallions

¼ cup raspberry

1 tbsp raw unfiltered honey

INSTRUCTIONS

1. Moisten the Nori to make it pliable. Chop the scallions.

2. Combine the tuna, extra virgin olive oil, dried mustard and chopped scallions and mix them together into a blend.

3. Spread the blend into each piece of Nori and wrap them up. Drizzle with honey and place raspberries on top. Serve.

Dragonchicken Wraps

Prep time: 15 minutes

Serves: 2

INGREDIENTS

6 slices organic grass-fed deli chicken

1 jalapeno

2 stalks celery

½ avocado

1 tbsp fresh basil

INSTRUCTIONS

1. Chop the jalapeno pepper and mash the avocado. Slice the celery into stalks that fit the diameter of a slice of deli chicken meat.

2. Stack 3 slices of deli chicken and spread the avocado mash across the middle. Place the celery through the center, sprinkle the basil across the middle and then evenly distribute the jalapeno slices. Wrap the chicken up and secure with toothpicks. Save enough of each ingredient to repeat this process across the other 3 slices of deli chicken. Serve.

Eggplant Chicken Burgers

Prep time: 15 minutes

Cook time: 8 minutes

Serves: 2

INGREDIENTS

Burger

1 eggplant

4 small organic grass-fed chicken breasts or thighs

1 tomato

1 onion

1 handful romaine lettuce

1 tbsp coconut oil

¼ tsp smoked paprika

Sauce

¼ packed cup fresh basil

2 tbsp extra virgin olive oil

1 clove garlic

2 tbsp walnuts

¼ tsp Celtic sea salt

INSTRUCTIONS

1. Combine the sauce ingredients in a food processor and puree.

2. Slice the eggplant into 8 round slices. Slice the tomato and onion into 4 slices each. Break the romaine lettuce up into smaller pieces.

3. Sprinkle the chicken with smoked paprika and combine with coconut oil in a small pan over medium heat. Sautee until cooked through and no longer pink, about 4 minutes on each side.

4. Assemble 4 burgers in the following manner: 1 slice eggplant, 1 piece chicken, 1 slice tomato, 1 slice onion, drizzled sauce, 1 slice eggplant. Secure with toothpick if desired. Serve 2 burgers to each person.

Chickenfish Wraps

Prep time:

Serves: 2

INGREDIENTS

6 slices organic grass-fed deli chicken

1 can tuna

2 tbsp extra virgin olive oil

½ tsp smoked paprika

½ avocado

INSTRUCTIONS

1. Mix tuna, extra virgin olive oil, smoked paprika and avocado into a paste.
2. Stack 3 slices of deli chicken and spread the paste across the diameter of the top. Wrap the chicken up and secure with toothpicks. Repeat for the other 3 slices and serve.

Mangospice Chicken Soup

Prep time: 15 minutes

Cook time: 45 minutes

Serves: 2

INGREDIENTS

2 cups organic vegetable stock

2 organic grass-fed chicken breasts

1 red bell pepper

1 yellow bell pepper

½ onion

1 clove garlic

1 cup mango

1 tbsp extra virgin olive oil

2 tbsp lemon juice

¼ tsp Celtic sea salt

¼ tsp ground black pepper

INSTRUCTIONS

- Cut the peppers in half. Remove the stems, cores and seeds. Line a baking sheet with aluminum foil and place the peppers in it skin side up. Put peppers under the broiler and leave them there until the skin has begun to turn black and shriveled.

- Remove peppers from oven, place in a plastic bag and place in refrigerator until cool.
- Peel the skins off the peppers and throw them away. Chop the peppers.
- Preheat oven to 350. Place chicken on a baking dish with extra virgin olive oil and lemon juice. Bake for 20 minutes or until chicken is no longer pink.
- Chop the onion and mango and crush the garlic.
- Place onion and garlic in a large saucepan with ½ cup vegetable stock and boil for 5 minutes. Add the rest of the stock and the roasted peppers and bring it back to a boil. Turn the heat down, cover, and let simmer for 5 minutes.
- Using an immersion blender, blend the contents of the saucepan. Chop up the cooked chicken and place it, along with the mango, in the saucepan.
- Season with sea salt and ground black pepper and heat through.
- Serve.

Earthroot Soup

Prep time: 5 minutes

Cook time: 15 minutes

Serves: 2

INGREDIENTS

½ quart organic vegetable stock

½ leek

1 cup celery root

3 oz fresh spinach

1 cup cauilfllower

¼ tsp Celtic sea salt

¼ tsp ground black pepper

¼ tsp nutmeg

1 ½ tsp grated fresh ginger

INSTRUCTIONS

1. Slice the leek and dice the celery root. Cut the cauliflower into florets.

2. Pour the vegetable stock in a saucepan and add the leeks, celery root, cauliflower florets, ginger and spinach. Bring to a boil.

Reduce heat and simmer for 10-15 minutes until vegetables are tender.

3. Using an immersion blender, blend the contents of the saucepan until pureed.

4. Season with Celtic sea salt, ground black pepper and nutmeg.

5. Serve.

Omelet Soup

Prep time: 5 minutes

Cook time: 18-20 minutes

Serves: 2

INGREDIENTS

1 oz organic grass-fed turkey bacon

2 cage-free eggs

½ onion

1 tbsp extra virgin olive oil

6 oz portabella mushrooms

1 ½ cups organic chicken stock

2 tsp Italian seasoning

2 springs of sage

¼ tsp Celtic sea salt

¼ tsp ground black pepper

INSTRUCTIONS

1. Chop the onion. Roughly chop the bacon and place it in a medium saucepan on medium heat. Cook through.

2. Add the onion and extra virgin olive oil and stir. Chop the mushrooms and add to the pan. Cover and cook for 2-3 minutes.

3. Add the chicken stock, seasoning, Celtic sea salt and ground black pepper to taste. Cover and simmer for 10 minutes.

4. Using an egg poacher if available, poach both eggs in the soup.

5. Serve and garnish with sage.

Trail Mix Soup

Prep time: 5-10 minutes

Cook time: 25-30 minutes

Serves 2:

INGREDIENTS

2 cups organic vegetable stock

1 oz coconut milk

½ red onion

1 heaping cup chopped sweet potato

1 apple

½ tsp ginger powder

2 tbsp extra virgin olive oil

¼ tsp cinnamon

1 tbsp chopped scallion

1 tbsp slivered almonds

¼ tsp Celtic sea salt

¼ tsp ground black pepper

2 tsp shredded coconut

INSTRUCTIONS

1. Mince the onion and slice and chop the apple.

2. In a medium saucepan, combine extra virgin olive oil and onion and cook over medium heat for 5 minutes.

3. Add sweet potato and apple and sautee for another 3 minutes.

4. Mix in ginger, cinnamon, scallion, Celtic sea salt and ground black pepper. Reduce heat to lowand sautee another 10 minutes, stirring occasionally.

5. Add vegetable stock and almonds and stir. Cover and simmer for 8-10 minutes until vegetables are soft.

6. Add coconut milk to soup and stir well.

7. Serve and garnish with shredded coconut.

Honeyfruit Soup

Prep time: 15 minutes

Serves: 2

INGREDIENTS

1 cantaloupe

1 cup sliced cooked beets

½ cup water

1 lime

1 tbsp shredded basil

basil leaves for garnishing

raw, organic honey for garnishing

INSTRUCTIONS

1. Slice the beets. Scrape out any seeds in the melon and throw away. Squeeze the juice out of the lime.

2. Using a melon baller scoop ten balls out of the cantaloupe. Leave at least one half of the cantaloupe untouched. Set aside for garnish.

3. Scoop out the rest of the cantaloupe and place in a blender or food processor. Add water, beets and lime juice and blend.

4. Transfer the mixture to a bowl, add the shredded basil and stir. Place in the refrigerator to chill for at least 30 minutes.

5. When serving, add 5 cantaloupe balls to each bowl and garnish with basil leaves and drizzle with honey.

Printed in Great Britain
by Amazon